Let's Hear It for the Horses

Tricia Knoll

Third Place Winner of The Poetry Box Chapbook Prize, 2021

Editing, Book & Cover Design: Shawn Aveningo Sanders
Cover Image: Sasha Fox Walters (iStock)
Author Photo was taken at Stead's Ranch, Estes Park, CO in 1958

ISBN: 978-1-956285-03-1
Printed in the United States of America.
Wholesale Distribution via Ingram.

Published by The Poetry Box®, February 2022
Portland, Oregon
ThePoetryBox.com

Cave art from 30,000 years ago reveals that horses intrigued early people. Humans partnered up with horses at least 5,000 years ago. Horses have plowed fields and pulled wagons. They participated in wars and learned to pirouette in show rings. We came to know horsepower. The people who love them learned gentling. Praise be to stablemates and wild horses on public rangelands and in Chernobyl.

The young girl in cowgirl boots who followed behind him riding over mountain passes and through roaring streams dedicates these poems to her father, Harry Walter Knoll. His relationship with Lucky spanned almost fifteen years.

Contents

Let's Hear It for the Horses

One million dead in the Civil War,
if you count the mules.
Which I do.

I say, blowtorch the rebel statue
men off their mounts and keep
the horses striding on their pedestals.

They were not traitors
to their country, showed no sign
of caring who they carried,

black or white, male or
female. Their integrity
is without question.

They did the work
they were asked to do
without a nod at glory.

Confluence

The cowboy entered on a gray horse. Wearing a white Stetson,
with tan hands, and tight jeans. He rode up to a Walmart
in Eagle Point, Oregon to buy dog food. He heard
a woman scream, pointing to a young man riding off
on her bike. The cowboy cantered after the bike thief,
threw his lasso, brought the kid down, tied him
to a tree and called a policeman who thought
the capture was totally slick.

I watched that video clip ten times.
I want that horse. I want to solve a problem
with an unexpected skill, a leap out of ordinary.
For twenty years I wore a silver Navajo bracelet
with three coral ovals—my Wonder Woman
cuff to deflect fear, absorb bad vibes and fight for freedom.
I love red boots, red slippers, red sandals
and if I can catch anything in my rope,
I'd aim for a glimmer of equality, of womanpower,
on a mare with an Appaloosa rump blanket of stars
who picked her way through the pass
marked with ancient carvings on rock
and heard voices in tall grasses.

If the woman who almost lost her bike is grateful
for horses, so am I. To remember Kapkap-Pommi,
(Noise of Running Feet), who at the age of twelve
galloped up to Sitting Bull's camp in Canada
ahead of U. S. soldiers pursuing her father,
the Nez Perce Chief Joseph, leading his people
through the freezing Bitterroots in an escape
toward Canada. He of fight-no-more-forever
surrender. He who was never permitted to return home.

She never saw her father in his exile.
When she returned to the states, she was renamed
Sarah and put in an agency boarding school. But first,
and always, she outwitted and outrode Colonel Miles'
white soldiers. That is why I love my bracelet
of possibility and unexpected endings.

Buddha's Stallion and the Woman
Who Married Wallace Stevens

Buddha's white stallion carried him from the palace
away from noble warrior games to jump over the river.
When Siddhartha tied the proud Kinthaka to a tree,
the young bridegroom fled for freedom, to roam
his path, and broke the loyal horse's heart.
A heart that returned after death as a follower.
This horse carved on stupas, painted, sketched—The Way
starts as a mounted man on a path out of town.

Elsie Stevens could have claimed *I am the woman
on the Liberty dime.* She never did. Historians
compared her image to a sculpture of her
that Adolph Weinman made at another time, stressed
that Stevens and Weinman lived in the same building.
Liberty's feathered cap for freedom of thought
on a wife who kept separate worlds, rooms apart,
strained and uncertain under his crystal chandeliers.

Supporting actors of heartbreak, those who wait,
who never shake loose of obligations and adorations. The rewards
of secondaries. Who they are. Who we each might be.

Cowboy Art in the University Library

Paintings with pale sky, wind-buffeted pines and loaded pack horses with wide rumps and blonde manes—ones just like these decorate ten thousand tavern walls. Or curl as calendars in filling stations in blow-away towns. Men in chaps slump over dollar-size belt buckles; their hats fold into conventions of cowboy. This artist painted a Navajo-red thunderbolt on one saddle blanket, an accent to trail-dust hues of boredom. What the armed horseback renegades who occupied the Malheur Refuge had in mind when riding out with an American flag for TV cameras.

  the kettling hawk
  a dive below the barb wire
  black-tailed jack rabbit

I smell horse dung. Hear bawls of cattle who stumble-walk so dozy their heads bob. Jingle of spurs, creaks of old leather. Horseshoe clicks on rock.

This picture frame is too narrow for an aging cowgirl. This birder finding Malheur's cranes through a spotting scope. This poet who cannot rhyme refuge with subterfuge.

  garden dirt
  under my fingernails
  burying bygones

Displayed in the children's library, the cowboys in black-and-white prints twist snakes into lariats and ride bounding waves on the backs of seals.

  woven baskets
  collect beautiful stones
  the spring water

Old Cowgirl's Rumination

Can I still sit the saddle
of the leathery past
that I never rode bareback?
My hand up to the mare's nose,

she blows back warmth.
I pick crud from mudded hooves
that once split thunder.
I comb out her winter coat

come May when always
May comes on time.
Her mane hair whirlpools
in barn wind.

She nickers to her buddies,
minces through the pasture gate,
trots to the levee. When shadows stretch,
she comes for my carrot.

Never having rode her bareback
doesn't matter now,
when she sniffs my palm,
her whiskers tickle.

The Switch

If I were a mare, an aging cow pony with a dark line down my back
when August's sun is so hot, I'd stand still in drying grasses
and curse the biting flies on my eyes that make me wish I could
fall asleep somewhere dark and cool where the water is fresh

And if you are the bay dressage thoroughbred in the same pasture
and you have a white cotton mask over your head and ears
and a light gauze fly sheet sprayed with deterrent herbal oils
on your back and that tasteless man beyond the fence says you look
like some kind of Ku Klux Horse though the flies still hover

And if you amble forward toward a hank of lushness
that grows out from under the split-rail fence,
if I saw a green stain of spit on your lip and the way
your skin flutters where flies land,
if I hear your hoof hit a rock and though you don't stumble,
you take three steps with a bit of hesitation between each,

then I would wander toward you; I might find
some wonderful mouthful on the way. Or not.
I don't care what your mask and blanket means
in terms of who cares for you and who cares for me

so I'd turn my rump toward your nose slowly
in the way of old ponies, and I would flick
my tail knowing you will switch at flies on me
because for all our years, no matter whether snow
drifts in the door to our barn or the water buckets
in our stalls are flecked with slimed hay and beetles,
no matter, we are stablemates, barn-naked side by side.

Hay Harvest in New Mexico

She and I smell gray-green.
West wind breathes life into pasture grass
mowed into tidy stripes.
How simple is harvest,

fall's clumping, a distraction
of gold and cider, last berries and spiders,
the death of dahlias, the dog's shed of summer.
The farmhand cranks up his baler. The rake lifts

dry hay scraped from silver dust.
He drags rows, makes rectangles
smaller and smaller inside themselves.
Then the baler extrudes perfect blocks.

On wood chairs below gold cottonwoods we share
strategies for the dialogue poem you wrote
to the woman who deserted you, kidnapped your dog
and stole what you believe was your last chance

at love. I note ambiguities of blame
you assign to mothers: yours who named
you for a nun and said nuns never lied,
hers who was careless with knives

and believed all her daughter's lies.
I suggest stanza breaks for each speaker.
Two men with a green truck stack bales
like books on a cart. You remove your glasses,

wipe them. Amid this dust of honest labor,
you weep. Their truck sways under its load.
I know where it goes. To barns sheltering
winter's steam-breathers, hope curling

from the nostrils of impatient horses,
and the tackling antics of restless goats
for a place at the manger. You apologize
for crying. The hay disappears down the road.

Winter Solstice in Vermont

Those Federal-style box homes boast
one electric candle in each window
to light a way through old stories.

Horses in muddy blankets walk
out on this December day to graze
on dirty-blonde pasture grass.
One pinto down the road
paws up patches in the thaw.

Soon they go inside to hay
and steam their heavy breath
tingled with chill in a red barn.

Nearby, two large teddy bears drive a red sleigh
unattached to anything in a cold field.

Unblanketed

The haunchy gold draft horse lowers down
in a stubbled winter pasture crusted in old snow,
rolls as if her itch has been in her for hours, waiting.
Around this fat mare lies January's truth,
winter lumbers half-way through
and offers only a moment's respite.

Browse

Horses love to graze and they do it now
in dirty blankets in a muddy field where
snippets of greening grass try to survive
the appetite of those who ate dry hay
all winter. Trailing their noses, seeking
the newest green blades—if horses know
that someone will arrive at five to urge
them back to stalls, they don't care
in this noon sun because of that taste,
first lush of April, free for deliberate taking.

Feel my need: the simplest chance
to touch the spines of hard-back books
sequestered in our town library,
to choose to move from hard fact to glancing
at poems women wrote to survive
long weeks inside, even Dickinson, or
kids' books where monkeys talk,
and ponies wear roller skates.
Where four gray-haired librarians
(why are they all women?) never judge
what I need (even smut), never ask
why I pick the book on how to fill lonely
hours. That forgiving date they stamp
on the fly leaf as they mention renewal
and point to hand sanitizer by the exit door.
At home, my nibble of what was free,
tangy taste of outside.

Heartbreak

He called it the foundering of a mighty white-winged horse,
limping through mossy damp. Wounded. Untamable.

He was wrong. There is no such thing as heartbreak.
The heart curdles, congeals, skedaddles in bad beats.

If it broke, we would die—
heartbreak is not so kind.

It gallops a deafening drum song
on open range without a saddle

or taps at windows with bony fingers,
but never, ever does it break open

the way love does.

The Poetry I Want

I'd like my poem to start with the shift of haunches
of humble draft horses clopping over cobblestones.
To go forward measured, steady. Or digress
on the translation of the Tibetan word for envy
as *heavy shoulders.* To sing out for the clergyman
who said that if we live for an eye for an eye,
the whole world goes blind. To announce a giant
in skirts come to straighten our folds of dismay.

Under my fingernail lurks dirt—winter weeding
when the seeds of what's not wanted have split open,
new sprouts almost controllable, both sadness
and envy. A few bees struggle out of the hive
this early February. One snowdrop opens.
Arctic winds could still deliver a kick,
the aikido master showing off. My only way
to hear clink on cobblestones is with my trowel,
my come-to-hand friend who excises the errant
to make room in rocky soil for the eyes
of acquiescent hellebores.

Summer Poetry Reading in the Courtyard
of What Was Once the Coach Barn
at Shelburne Farms

A woman in an apricot dress plays Dvorak on her violin.
Can you hear warmblood haunches shift against wood stalls?

One poet describes his bumpy ride in a bi-plane over these green acres.
A carriage horse stomps metal shoes on yellow brick.

Another poet looks over the side of a green canoe into the LaPlatte River
and remembers his mother.

Under the big clock over the doorway to the harnessing hall,
I hear echoes of what mattered—

Tired bay saddlebreds nickered to each other in generous stalls.
the stablehands' halloo-ed and *Move over, Bridey,*

I've got fresh water and your mash.
Don't fret the poets. They're from another time.

"That Is Someone Else's Story"

The social worker's gossip
galloped out of the barn door
to stomp hock-deep in spring-muck pasture,
flick its mane, hoist a hoof to kick
its neighbor in the gut, and hunker in the rain.

Then she threw out these words
borrowed from the Inuit.

My Unforgettable House

This wood playhouse couldn't hold a horse, so we tied
our mares to the oak tree outside with no-nonsense
reins of imagination that kept the steeds
pawing the earth until we walked out

the doorless front, me waving
the white dishcloth that doubled as a curtain
for windows on the back, held in place
by thumb tacks beside the whisk broom

we used to sweep the dirt floor
below the wooden crate that held
the tiny tea dishes and the spoons,
where there must have been spiders

in the split-log crevices that showed sunlight
spilled from the lilacs in the back
but we weren't just girls then,
we were mothers, ranchers, herders

with hard work to do conjuring
up the next adventure in our wild,
frantic mounting of our rides
to chase away the bears

that might emerge from the corn field
or finding acorn caps for dishes
and sticks for riding crops.
We never slept or napped

in this rustic cabin. Each had a say
about where things went,
my say louder than others
in that happy house.

Cantering the Air Horse

I rode my prancing pony only on the west side of the block.
Mounting at the oaks corner, beyond Nancy's picture window.
The wide, untended parkway beside the gravel road
extended to the little woods where I cantered with fisted reins,
a quarter horse of different color every summer day.

I chose the trail through boulders, picking
our way to the oak sapling that bled from a pruning wound.
My horse stood, reins dangling. I picked up my stowed twig,
and spread dripping sap, care for healing, care for smelling
sticky on my hand.

At the next corner I left my horse, continuing clockwise (always),
through noon sun. The Jacobsen's German Shepherds barked,
pushing against the wire, streaming back and forth,
kenneled. This side of the block, the Illinois sun cooked the pavement.
I walked then, a girl I know lived here. Her mother sometimes
made her ask me over to play. She and her friends did not canter,
never nickered or blew out full lips. Mickey might come down
his driveway, tell my brothers I was riding around again.

Near driveway #7, no trees cast shadows.
I don't think I had one. It was too hot for shade.
At the Cordell's house, I might pick a rosebud,
a little yellow one, in theory for my mother.
She would not approve of stealing roses,
and she did not like horses.

After Winning the Horse Race at Age Eleven

You did not eat dirt today.
Perhaps tomorrow. Victory
is one thin nacre coat
on one grain of effort.
Remember the mare's beauty.
She sweat more than you did.

Look ahead to kittens and dogs
and the feasts of wild crows.
These too know the roll of dirt.
All the living taste
dust and simple sun.

To Talk of Gold

This story has me on a plodder mare
from a rental stable, a horse for a little girl
to ride deep-dust trails in Estes Park.
Eight hours to Long Lake and back.
I follow my father on his sorrel named
Lucky.

Horse-mad, I kick my cowgirl boots
on a horse that would not trot
and never away from the barn.
A nameless paint I loved.

Hours into dry pines, picking
our way down a full-sun ridge
studded with boulders and columbine
gone to seed, Lucky starts prancing,
nickers. My paint jingles and sidesteps.
I wake from a rocking doziness.
My father pulls up. Bits clang.
Horsey nerves make the saddles creak.

A cougar on one granite boulder looks
down on us, hunches, leaps and stretches
over us across the trail into August's
tall dry grass. Tawny gold into gold.
Slow-motion gone to gold.

May nothing take my breath away
again like this pure wild gold
until the dangerous day I die.

My Father's Old Road

Packed in with promises of not to fight,
two brothers and I on red leather seats
of a 1950s Buick Wildcat convertible,
headed west from Chicago every August.

Ride-alongs on my father's trip,
top down under the Iowa-then-Nebraska sky
sometimes heat on, windows up against cold
rushing to Colorado.

Always, always that top down,
   open sky blowing
   mother's hair matted in some straw hat
      studded with turquoise charms
 and red cloth straps tied under her chin.

There were many things I didn't know—
      how my brothers felt sitting so close together
      why my father's thinning scalp never sunburned
      why he lifted his chin sideways to the sun
      why we couldn't sing 99 Bottles of Beer
      why we had to have the top down all the way
         to peach pie at the red brick hotel in North Platte

and I still don't know
      how to see time passing in a sliding sky
      what's to mourn in perfect loss
      and why we kids stared straight up into blue
         when told we'd be somewhere soon.

I did know my father's fixation
with old roads. My father pointed out
every old road oxbow hidden in the cottonwoods.

He never noted the stink of pig farms,
the circling of hawks or the height of corn.
Just old roads paralleling the Platte,
old roads bending through Loveland Pass,
rock tunnels built for prospectors
mining the mountains, not our Wildcat.

Then that trail to Cub Lake in Estes Park,
twenty years after the first trip west.

That day he went alone on horseback—
his Wildcat and my mother in her ticking shirt
back at the Y-Camp stable; he giddy-upped
the old sorrel gelding, Lucky, saying to wranglers:
 It's a day made in heaven.

His was.

Two backpackers found him sprawled
face up in trail dust, dead
under Lucky's dangling reins,
this old road where he stared
his awe at a blue wide-open topless
Colorado mountain sky.

Where I Rest My Horse

We trust each other
to share cool water from a stream,
not missing buckets hung on stout nails.
No clock, no calendar, no news
shakes the solid clay and greenish grass
underneath our feet. No smoke.

The wind's whisper-strength seems lonesome
as it touches drying sweat. The sun shows
intent to set in degrees, unrushed.

We have worked and needn't now.
Dusk seems as simple as nearby grazing.
fresh water, soft snorts,
and an indifferent sky
without agenda.
Is that sobbing downstream?
We are unsure.

We amble.
Even the milkweed
seed dallies as magic
and the rocks in the water
stand still for an overflow,
generous and silent.

Neither of us notices
who watches out for the other.

To My Father

I was so young
when you died.
You knew I had the body
of a woman and fears of a girl.

You never knew I stole
quarters from your dresser.
You liked your handkerchiefs
pressed, to cheer Big 10 football games,
a quartered apple after dinner,
and vegetable soup on Sunday evenings.
You took me to the rodeos and to see
the Lipizzans.

You believed everything would turn out
for the best even though it took me
weeks to learn to drive a clutch.

I was so young when you died riding
up a mountain pass. I knew no German
words for love. What I have left of you
is one broken compass, a letter to me
you dictated to your secretary,
and confidence a gentled horse never kicks or bites,
that gentling is a touch of palm to withers
that brings a warm breath
to my outstretched hand.

The Mare's Eye

Rest your nervous eye, my blinking beauty.
My hand comes up slow to your nostrils
so you take in the all of me,
the all of me that seeks to nuzzle your cheek,
the whole that knows how we soothe
each other, the soft tips of your ears
turned to consider trust of my low shushes.

I am not predator, and for this moment
you are not herd, not chased, not pushed
to go anywhere except into the quiet
rustle of hay where mice nest
in the straw and the gray barn cat
curls its tail against the sliding door.

You know this,
over and over
how we gentle each other.

One-Hundred Yards from the Dude Ranch Corral in New Mexico

This close the smell of cut hay, horse piss and manure
fits in with the rust on a four-horse trailer and the brown paint
of the round pen and corral. The wrangler on a palomino
leads back three girls on horseback wearing shiny helmets.
Their bays plod the sand and gravel road, ears perked
to the smell of alfalfa at their barn.

A Swedish woman came by an hour ago to book a ride.
I told her she had to do that at the office over the hill
from the cell phone tower. We discovered that both
our mothers had hated horses; hers was newly dead.
She wanted to ride to be less like her mother.

I'd long ago given over to horse love learned from my father.
In the corral a bay and a black, two old boys whose spines
sway down, stand cheek to rump and rump to cheek
to swat each other's flies. I wait for my hair to dry
beneath an apple tree where birds ate the top half
of every apple and no apple smell scents the desert air.

I doubt the motherless woman will be back
next summer. The old geldings will go out to pasture.
I'm finishing up my work in this red rock landscape.
That leaves the old tin barn roof to hold the weather
and the apple tree to know what it knows.

Jack

I walk to the corral to kick at burden-blues in gravel,
nudge aside stuttered stones on a rutted road.

There is Jack, a retired cowpony, with gray age-spots
and the sharp backbone ridge of a smart horse

who had sorted cows, rode fences, twisted around barrels.
Now munching sweet grain to keep weight on his rump.

I sidle behind him with a dandy brush,
curry out dirt, scrubbing circles,

bring up the dust of trail rides on a dude ranch,
miles of hoof clicks to rocks bigger than my fist.

I swipe his hooves, mud sucked from some sluggish creek
while we loitered in gold pasture grass heavy with seed

and wished for us a bigger arena.
He stands collected under my brush,

content to watch others get saddled up.
I wipe away fly crust near his eyes,

as if he had waited all through lunch for this.
My eyes need clarity.

The wind holds us, hot to a flick of his swivel ears,
a reason for my roaming long hair to shed onto Jack

and the dust of his bay coat to turn my right hand gray,
my left respecting his solidity of hip.

The wrangler said not to mind Jack's battle scars,
the hairless spot mid-back, that gray-black scab

[. . .]

where a saddle scored his spine.
Jack is a good boy, she said, *full of spunk.*

His head-down serenity under my touch,
his gas passed, a lean to my brush.

He was all cowponies, now he is not one
but with me also one.

Catch & Release

The trout fisherman's poem flew in by email today.
Why he thinks trout bite, why he lets them go.

Next in line the neighbor's plea—a golden lab puppy
ran out the back door with a blue collar and a romping thirst.

That fly Obama caught in his fist,
a grab others try and mostly fail.

We are catchers. We net.
We trap elephants. Able now and then

to lean a cheek against the bay gelding's withers
and say *big heart, go,*

run for all you are worth
while I lean on this fractured fence,

hold your halter,
and sing how beautiful you are.

Yard Art

Winter knocked the angel silly,
my companion in isolation.
The metal goddess with a stone head
leans back and a long-needled pine
bough drapes over her shoulder, itch
on simple lines.

Rusty took a harder hit. My bent rebar
life-size horse. He fell sideways twice
in a thaw, four legs out stiff like that
dead horse bobbing in the waves
off Pacific Beach. He weighs more
than one old woman can easily
resurrect, poor old gelding, but
I got him up and his legs pushed
into mud deep enough to stand
up to April showers. Probably long
enough that I won't need to worry
about him until fall's winds. Maybe—

I'm looking for a flea market
saddle to strap on him.
To go with his muzzle mask.
When they postponed the Derby,
I cut out red paper roses, draped him
end-of-winter winner.

After the Mare Finishes Jumping

A hand holds out a cookie of molasses and oats.
Square in the center of that little cake,
red or black licorice or a peppermint.

Job well done. Time for rest
and health care, cool water,
baths, consideration
for overtime, a refuge
with a solid roof,
greens, a kind hand,
good neighbors,
legal papers,
retirement benefits
and a living wage.

Racing

Twenty years ago a Chicago Marathon race director
stood behind a chair in a bar, showing how he steered his dog team
in the Iditarod. He swerved the chair, clucked his tongue, flexed
his knees. His move to marathon racing? There's joy
in the way creatures run. Life overflows. Joy
in how good people tend to good creatures.

And Turcotte. That small jockey on the big red horse,
the impossibly big-hearted horse and the 1973 Triple Crown.
When I saw Haley's comet in 1986, I knew
it was a once in a lifetime the way my years fall.
I feared so it might go with the Triple Crown.
Never another Turcotte on a Secretariat?

Bless Seattle Slew, Affirmed, American Pharoah,
Justify—those well-tendeds who ran
for their owners, ran for their trainers, ran to remind us
of that big red horse that swept the field.
Love how they run.
Joy in how good people tend good creatures.

Then Turcotte. Rolling on wheels in a chair
after a car accident. Churchill Downs could not save
an accessible place for him to park.
His chair, his heart. His legacy
with that big red horse. Apologies
placing last.

Roll Call

Blue 🐎 Secretariat 🐎 blue ribbon 🐎 Daisy 🐎 Mr. Ed

Of course! Of course! 🐎 Houyhnhnm 🐎 National Velvet

the mare who opens her mouth for a bit 🐎 Flicka 🐎 Jack

Bucephalus 🐎 dusty trail to Bear Lake 🐎 wild mustangs

my father splashed us through streams at a trot 🐎 Misty 🐎

Sultana 🐎 Seattle Slew 🐎 Pegasus 🐎 Trigger 🐎

Black Beauty & Ginger & Merrylegs 🐎 Seabiscuit 🐎

Breyer horse glued on the mailbox 🐎 King of the Wind 🐎

Beanie Babies & My Little Ponies 🐎 Snowy River brumbies

Mother's Day brush outs 🐎 Rex 🐎 Silver 🐎

we called the Budweiser Clydesdales "shoe shoes" 🐎

Lipizzans in Chicago 🐎 saddle sore 🐎 Sham 🐎

Tennessee Stud 🐎 Maamin 🐎 Brighty 🐎 Blaze

pricked ears & steel shoes 🐎 American Pharoah 🐎 nag

Ino A. Horse 🐎 bareback 🐎 whoa 🐎 dismount

Unbridled

When the day comes
for my ghost ride,

I'll snatch the black mane
of that bay mare that won
the race for my Tourmaline team

       I cling to the camp's fastest quarter horse,
       strike out around the bend
       to the grandstand
       of that weathered Buena Vista rodeo track,
       silting those Garnet and Topaz riders stuck behind

her to win,
me to hang on.

I'll jump with her, rise up,
the two of us stringing

       dark mare tail
       my long braid

snagging in the grasping sticks
of naked trees, a gallop up
the haggard slice of ice moon

       feeling our heat
       stampeding feet
       on nimbus turf.

In the End

It wasn't Lucky
or my friend's thirty-two-year-old mare,
part Tennessee Walker, part Arab
who made me write this

or Darcy, the paint in the rodeo photo
or Secretariat, or Daisy who won
the quarter-mile race

but gratitude for sharing
a universe with creatures
that inspired the Greeks,
Chinese, Hindi, followers
of Mohammed, Koreans,
Tibetans, Mongolians,
Assyrians and the Valkyries
to name the wind drinkers,
spirit and ghost horses—

and record visions of horses with wings,
hope
that we may rise above limits
with friends
different from us

Acknowledgments

Grateful acknowledgment is made to the editors of the journals and anthologies who first published the following poems—some in slightly different versions or with other titles.

Califragile: "Browse"

Calyx: "My Father's Old Road"

Full of Crow: "Buddha's Stallion and the Woman Who Married Wallace Stevens"

Gyroscope Review: "The Cowgirl's Rumination"

Mojave River Review: "Jack"

New Verse News: "After the Mare Finishes Jumping," "Let's Hear It for the Horses," "Racing"

Verse Virtual: "Catch & Release," "Confluence," "The Switch"

Visitant Lit: "After Winning the Horse Race at Age Eleven"

Visual Verse: "The Mare's Eye"

Praise for
Let's Hear It for the Horses

If you know your totem animal is Horse, you'll see these gentle giants everywhere—in the history of war, on gas-station calendars, haunting memories of harvest, a father's fall, and your own hand's memory of dusty withers. These poems will take you into a life enhanced by horses, as every life should be by something friendly but not defeated.

—Kim Stafford, author of *Singer Come from Afar*
Oregon Poet Laureate Emeritus

It's a great pleasure to browse this collection, just as Tricia Knoll's horses browse the field, looking for new, green blades of grass. She writes in the fine tradition of Maxine Kumin, and like that earlier poet, even has a poem for a horse named "Jack". Full of the breathtaking observations of the horse lover, Knoll takes the reader close to real and imagined horses—close enough to feel the tickle of their whiskers or notice the green spit on their lips. She also shares stories of the father who died before she was grown, but who guided her into life by taking her as a child on trail rides, or to see the Lipizzaner horses. You don't have to know horses to love these poems; they can serve as a generous introduction to the joy and sadness that canters in the air beside them.

—Judith Barrington, author
Long Love: New & Selected Poems, 1985–2017

This book, with craft and saddles and the warm breath, takes me into my past, one horse-girl to another. Tricia Knoll has found her inspiration on horseback, in the giddy-up, and *the pure wild gold, until the dangerous day I die.* The naming of horses in "Roll Call" just about takes my breath away.

—Joan Logghe, Santa Fe Poet Laureate Emerita

About the Author

"A horse. A horse. My kingdom for a horse!" cried King Richard the Third. Tricia Knoll's father thought this as a child until his practical father detailed the costs and suggested he rent one. Which he did, at Colorado dude ranches. On weekends in suburban Chicago to ride hell bent on trails through cornfields. Her father did everything he could to make sure Knoll loved horses too. Summer horse camps. Riding with her dad in Rocky Mountain National Park summer after summer. Sometimes riding at mad gallops with the suburban men. Horse shows and rodeos. He was at his best in his cowboy boots and pearl snap-button Western shirts.

Knoll has degrees in literature from Stanford University (BA) and Yale University (MAT). She taught high school English. Edited a newspaper for elementary students. Served as Public Relations Director for Portland, Oregon's Children's Museum. Acted as the Public Information Officer at the Portland Water Bureau and went to New Orleans as an emergency responder following Hurricane Katrina.

Knoll retired in 2007 to write. Her poetry collections address interactions of wildlife and humans in urban habitat (*Urban Wild*); people and creatures on an organic farm in Washington State (*Broadfork Farm*); change in a small town on Oregon's northern coast (*Ocean's Laughter*); her understanding of white privilege (*How I Learned To Be White*); and relationships that sometimes go askew (*Checkered Mates*). *How I Learned to Be White* received the 2018 Human Rights Indie Book Award for Motivational Poetry. She is a contributing editor to the online journal *Verse Virtual*.

[. . .]

Knoll lives in the woods of Vermont. Stables for dressage horses, a herd of pintos, and a one-horse family barn are less than a quarter mile in any direction. She smells them on warm days.

<triciaknoll.com>

The Poetry Box Chapbook Prize

The Poetry Box® Chapbook Prize is open to both established poets and emerging talent alike. The contest is open to poets residing in the United States and is open for submissions each year during the month of February. Find more information at ThePoetryBox.com.

2021 Winners:

Erasures of My Coming Out (Letter) by Mary Warren Foulk

Of the Forest by Linda Ferguson

Let's Hear It for the Horses by Tricia Knoll

2020 Winners:

The Day of My First Driving Lesson by Tiel Aisha Ansari

My Mother Never Died Before by Marcia B. Loughran

Off Coldwater Canyon by C.W. Emerson

2019 Winners:

Moroccan Holiday by Lauren Tivey

Hello, Darling by Christine Higgins

Falling into the River by Debbie Hall

2018 Winners:

Shrinking Bones by Judy K. Mosher

November Quilt by Penelope Scambly Schott

14: Antología del Sonoran by Christopher Bogart

Fireweed by Gudrun Bortman